Cocktails

Publications International, Ltd.

ISBN-13: 978-1-4508-5949-3
ISBN-10: 1-4508-5949-6

Library of Congress Control Number: 2012939688

Manufactured in China.

8 7 6 5 4 3 2 1

Publications International, Ltd.

TABLE OF CONTENTS

Campari Cooler, p. 32

Caipirinha, p. 6

Screwdriver, p. 12

CLASSIC COCKTAILS

Some things never go out of style—think Martinis, Gimlets, Sidecars and Stingers, to name just a few. Trends and fashions may change, but these drinks remain timeless.

Dirty Martinis

Screwdriver

Caipirinha

½ lime, cut into wedges
4 teaspoons sugar
2 ounces cachaça*

*A Brazilian brandy. Substitute any brandy, if necessary.

Combine lime wedges and sugar in old fashioned glass; muddle with wooden spoon. Fill glass with crushed ice; add cachaça.

Caipiroska: Substitute vodka for cachaça.

Caipirissima: Substitute rum for cachaça.

Lime Rickey

2 ounces vodka
2 ounces gin
2 ounces lime juice
   Club soda
   Lime wedge

Fill cocktail glass with ice; pour vodka, gin and lime juice over ice. Fill with club soda. Garnish with lime wedge.

Raspberry Rickey: Place ⅓ cup raspberries in small bowl; sprinkle with 2 teaspoons sugar. Add lime juice; let sit 10 minutes. Press through sieve to remove seeds. Combine raspberry mixture, 2 ounces raspberry-flavored vodka and 2 ounces gin in ice-filled old fashioned glass. Fill with club soda. Garnish with fresh raspberries and mint leaves.

Caipirinha

Americano

1½ ounces sweet vermouth
1½ ounces Campari
   Chilled club soda
   Lemon wedge or slice

Fill old fashioned glass or highball glass with ice. Pour vermouth and Campari over ice; fill with club soda. Garnish with lemon wedge.

Negroni

1 ounce gin
1 ounce Campari
1 ounce sweet or dry vermouth
   Lemon twist

Fill cocktail shaker half full with ice; add gin, Campari and vermouth. Stir until blended; strain into chilled cocktail glass. Garnish with lemon twist.

Campari is an Italian drink made from infusing bitter herbs, aromatic plants and fruits in alcohol and water. It is bright red in color with a strong aroma and distinctly bitter flavor. Campari is most commonly mixed with club soda and served over ice, but it is also an ingredient in several classic cocktails.

Americano

Buck

Juice of ¼ lime
1½ ounces gin
Ginger ale
Lemon twist or slice

Fill old fashioned glass with ice; squeeze lime juice over ice and drop lime into glass. Add gin; fill with ginger ale. Garnish with lemon twist.

Gin & Tonic

2 ounces gin
4 ounces tonic water
Lime wedge

Fill old fashioned glass with ice; pour gin over ice. Stir in tonic. Garnish with lime wedge.

Pisco Sour

2 ounces pisco brandy
1 ounce lime juice
¼ ounce simple syrup*
½ egg white
1 dash Angostura bitters

To make simple syrup, bring 1 cup water to a boil; stir in 1 cup sugar. Reduce heat to low; stir constantly until sugar is dissolved. Cool syrup to room temperature; store in glass jar in refrigerator.

Fill cocktail shaker half full with ice; add pisco, lime juice, simple syrup and egg white. Shake until blended; strain into chilled cocktail glass. Sprinkle foam with bitters.

Buck

Bloody Mary

Worcestershire sauce, hot pepper sauce, celery salt, black pepper and salt
1½ ounces vodka
3 ounces tomato juice
½ ounce lemon juice
Celery stalk with leaves, pickle spear, lemon slice and/or green olives

Fill highball glass with ice; add dashes of Worcestershire, hot pepper sauce, celery salt, black pepper and salt to taste. Add vodka, tomato juice and lemon juice; stir gently. Serve with desired garnishes.

Screwdriver

2 ounces vodka
6 ounces orange juice (¾ cup)
Orange slice

Fill old fashioned glass or highball glass half full with ice; pour vodka over ice. Stir in orange juice. Garnish with orange slice.

Bloody Mary

Sidecar

2 ounces brandy or Cognac
2 ounces orange liqueur
½ ounce lemon juice

Fill cocktail shaker half full with ice; add brandy, liqueur and lemon juice. Shake until blended; strain into chilled martini glass.

Delmonico

1 ounce gin
½ ounce brandy
½ ounce dry vermouth
½ ounce sweet vermouth
2 dashes Angostura bitters
Lemon twist

Fill cocktail shaker half full with ice; add gin, brandy, vermouths and bitters. Shake until blended; strain into chilled martini glass. Drop in lemon twist.

Angostura bitters are the most popular and most concentrated bitters available. They are used as a key flavoring agent in many cocktails, usually just a few drops or dashes at a time. (Since Angostura bitters are 90 proof—about 45% alcohol—they are rarely drunk straight.) Like other bitters, Angostura is made from roots, berries, herbs and plants, but the recipe has remained a secret since it was developed in the 1800s.

Sidecar

Sazerac

2 ounces whiskey
¼ ounce anise liqueur
½ ounce simple syrup*
   Dash bitters
   Lemon peel strip

*To make simple syrup, bring 1 cup water to a boil; stir in 1 cup sugar. Reduce heat to low; stir constantly until sugar is dissolved. Cool syrup to room temperature; store in glass jar in refrigerator.

Fill cocktail shaker half full with ice; add whiskey, liqueur, simple syrup and bitters. Stir until blended; strain into old fashioned glass. Garnish with lemon peel.

Old Fashioned

1 sugar cube*
2 dashes Angostura bitters
1 teaspoon water
2 ounces whiskey
   Lemon twist
   Orange slice and maraschino cherry

*Or use 2 teaspoons sugar syrup. Stir together syrup, bitters and water in glass.

Place sugar cube, bitters and water in old fashioned glass; muddle until sugar is dissolved. Add ice cubes; stir in whiskey and lemon twist. Garnish with orange slice and maraschino cherry.

Sazerac

Classic Dry Martini

2 ounces gin or vodka
½ ounce dry vermouth

Fill cocktail shaker half full with ice; add gin and vermouth. Stir or shake until blended; strain into chilled martini glass.

Dirty Martini: Add 1 to 2 teaspoons olive brine; garnish with olive.

Gibson: Garnish with cocktail onion.

Rolls Royce

1½ ounces gin
½ ounce dry vermouth
½ ounce sweet vermouth
½ teaspoon Bénédictine

Fill cocktail shaker half full with ice; add gin, vermouths and Bénédictine. Stir until blended; strain into chilled cocktail glass.

All vermouths are made from white wines and may be served on their own as apéritifs. Dry vermouth is used in dry cocktails such as martinis, while sweet vermouth, with a slightly sweet flavor and reddish-brown color, is used in sweeter cocktails like Negronis and Manhattans. Vermouth can be stored in the refrigerator for three to six months—the wine will not go bad after this time, but the flavor will dissipate.

Dirty Martinis

Kir

½ ounce crème de cassis (black currant liqueur)
¾ cup chilled dry white wine

Pour crème de cassis into white wine glass; pour in white wine.

Kir Royale: Replace white wine with chilled champagne or dry sparkling wine; serve in champagne flute.

Stinger

2 ounces brandy
¾ ounce white crème de menthe

Fill cocktail shaker half full with ice; add brandy and crème de menthe. Shake until blended; strain into chilled martini glass.

Shirley Temple

8 ounces ginger ale (1 cup)
1 ounce grenadine
Orange slice and maraschino cherry

Fill highball glass half full with ice; top with ginger ale and grenadine. Garnish with orange slice and maraschino cherry.

Kir Royale

Manhattan

2 ounces whiskey
1 ounce sweet vermouth
Dash Angostura bitters
Maraschino cherry

Fill cocktail shaker half full with ice; add whiskey, vermouth and bitters. Stir until blended; strain into chilled martini glass or old fashioned glass. Garnish with maraschino cherry.

Metropolitan

1½ ounces brandy
1½ ounces sweet vermouth
½ teaspoon simple syrup*
Dash bitters
Maraschino cherry

*To make simple syrup, bring 1 cup water to a boil; stir in 1 cup sugar. Reduce heat to low; stir constantly until sugar is dissolved. Cool syrup to room temperature; store in glass jar in refrigerator.

Fill cocktail shaker half full with ice; add brandy, vermouth, simple syrup and bitters. Shake until blended; strain into chilled martini glass. Garnish with maraschino cherry.

Manhattan

Bellini

3 ounces peach nectar*
4 ounces chilled champagne or dry sparkling wine
   Peach slice

Or peel and pit 1 ripe medium peach; purée in blender.

Pour peach nectar into chilled champagne flute; slowly add champagne. Garnish with peach slice.

Mimosa

4 ounces chilled orange juice
4 ounces chilled champagne

Pour orange juice into champagne flute; top with champagne.

Pimm's Cup

2 ounces Pimm's No. 1
   Lemon-lime soda
   Cucumber strip or spear
   Lemon twist

Fill chilled highball glass with ice; pour in Pimm's. Fill with lemon-lime soda. Garnish with cucumber strip and lemon twist.

Bellini

Gimlet

2 ounces gin
1 ounce lime juice
1 ounce simple syrup*
Lime slice or wedge

To make simple syrup, bring 1 cup water to a boil; stir in 1 cup sugar. Reduce heat to low; stir constantly until sugar is dissolved. Cool syrup to room temperature; store in glass jar in refrigerator.

Fill cocktail shaker half full with ice; add gin, lime juice and simple syrup. Shake until blended; strain into chilled martini glass. Garnish with lime slice.

Rob Roy

1½ ounces Scotch or any whiskey
¼ ounce sweet vermouth
Dash bitters
Maraschino cherry

Fill cocktail shaker half full with ice; add Scotch, vermouth and bitters. Shake until blended; strain into chilled martini glass. Garnish with maraschino cherry.

Gimlet

Snake Bite

8 ounces ale
8 ounces cider

Pour ale into chilled pilsner glass or pint glass; add cider (do not stir).

Half-and-Half

8 ounces ale
8 ounces porter

Pour ale into chilled pint glass. Pour porter over back of spoon on top of ale (do not stir).

Boilermaker

1 ounce whiskey
1 pint beer

Pour whiskey into shot glass. Pour beer into chilled pint glass. Drink whiskey first, followed by beer.

Depth Charge: Pour 1 ounce whiskey into chilled pint glass; fill with beer.

Snake Bites

Harvey Wallbanger

3 ounces vodka
6 ounces orange juice (¾ cup)
1 ounce Galliano
Orange slice or wedge

Fill highball glass half full with ice; pour vodka over ice. Stir in orange juice. Float Galliano on top; do not stir. Garnish with orange slice.

Tom Collins

2 ounces gin
1 ounce lemon juice
1 teaspoon superfine sugar
3 ounces club soda
Orange slice and maraschino cherry

Fill cocktail shaker half full with ice; add gin, lemon juice and sugar. Shake until blended; strain into ice-filled Collins glass. Top with club soda. Garnish with orange slice and maraschino cherry.

Galliano is a sweet Italian herbal liqueur that is packaged in a very distinctive tall, narrow bottle. It has a bright yellow color and thick, syrupy texture.

Harvey Wallbangers

Campari Cooler

1 ounce Campari
1 ounce peach schnapps
2 ounces orange juice
Juice of 1 lime (about 1½ tablespoons)
Club soda or lemon-lime soda (optional)
Orange wedge and maraschino cherry

Fill cocktail shaker half full with ice; add Campari, schnapps, orange juice and lime juice. Shake until blended; strain into ice-filled margarita or highball glass. Top with splash of club soda, if desired. Garnish with orange wedge and maraschino cherry.

Sloe Gin Fizz

1 ounce sloe gin
1 ounce gin
1 ounce simple syrup*
¾ ounce lemon juice
Club soda
Orange slice and maraschino cherry

*To make simple syrup, bring 1 cup water to a boil; stir in 1 cup sugar. Reduce heat to low; stir constantly until sugar is dissolved. Cool syrup to room temperature; store in glass jar in refrigerator.

Fill cocktail shaker half full with ice; add sloe gin, gin, simple syrup and lemon juice. Shake until blended; strain into ice-filled highball glass. Fill with club soda. Garnish with orange slice and maraschino cherry.

Campari Cooler

SHAKEN OR STIRRED

Add a little pizzazz to your next party with a Singapore Sling, Mojito or Cosmopolitan—these sophisticated sippers offer fresh flavors to please every palate.

Lemon Drop

Kamikaze

Cosmopolitan

2 ounces vodka or lemon-flavored vodka
1 ounce triple sec
1 ounce cranberry juice
½ ounce lime juice
   Lime wedge or slice

Fill cocktail shaker half full with ice; add vodka, triple sec, cranberry juice and lime juice. Shake until blended; strain into chilled martini glass. Garnish with lime slice.

Tip: For extra flair, serve in a sugar-frosted glass. Moisten the rim of a chilled glass with cranberry juice, then dip it into a saucer of granulated sugar.

Debonair

2½ ounces Scotch or whiskey
1 ounce ginger liqueur
   Lemon twist

Fill cocktail shaker half full with ice; add Scotch and liqueur. Shake until blended; strain into chilled martini glass. Garnish with lemon twist.

Cosmopolitan

Mojito

4 fresh mint leaves
1 ounce fresh lime juice
1 teaspoon superfine sugar or powdered sugar
1½ ounces light rum
    Soda water
    Fresh mint sprig and lime wedges

Muddle mint leaves, lime juice and sugar in highball glass; add 4 ice cubes. Pour rum over ice; fill with soda water. Garnish with mint sprig and lime wedges.

Kamikaze

1 ounce vodka
1 ounce triple sec
½ ounce blue curaçao (optional)
1 ounce lime juice
    Lemon slice

Fill cocktail shaker half full with ice; add vodka, triple sec, curaçao, if desired, and lime juice. Shake until blended; strain into chilled martini glass, large shot glass or ice-filled old fashioned glass. Garnish with lime slice.

Superfine sugar, also called bar sugar or castor sugar, is simply granulated sugar that is ground very fine. (It is *not* the same as powdered sugar.) Superfine sugar is often used in drinks because it dissolves quickly and easily in cold liquids. It can be found in the supermarket packaged in small boxes, or you can make your own by blending granulated sugar in a blender or food processor until powdery.

Mojitos

Brandy Alexander

2 ounces brandy
1 ounce dark crème de cacao
1 ounce half-and-half
¼ teaspoon ground nutmeg

Fill cocktail shaker half full with ice; add brandy, crème de cacao and half-and-half. Shake until blended; strain into chilled martini glass. Sprinkle with nutmeg.

Chocolate Martini

2 ounces vodka or vanilla-flavored vodka
1½ ounces crème de cacao
Chocolate shavings and maraschino cherry

Fill cocktail shaker half full with ice; add vodka and crème de cacao. Shake until blended; strain into chilled martini glass. Garnish with chocolate shavings and maraschino cherry.

Mint Chocolate Martini: Add ½ ounce crème de menthe to cocktail shaker.

White Chocolate Martini: Substitute white chocolate liqueur for crème de cacao.

Brandy Alexander

Amaretto Stone Sour

2 ounces amaretto liqueur
2 ounces sweet and sour mix
2 ounces orange juice
 Orange slice and maraschino cherry

Fill old fashioned glass or highball glass with ice; pour amaretto over ice. Stir in sour mix and orange juice. Garnish with orange slice and maraschino cherry.

Amaretto Sour: Increase amaretto and sweet and sour mix to 3 ounces each; omit orange juice. Prepare as directed above.

White Lady

2 ounces gin
1 ounce orange liqueur
½ ounce lemon juice

Fill cocktail shaker half full with ice; add gin, liqueur and lemon juice. Shake until blended; strain into chilled martini glass.

Sweet and sour mix is made of sugar syrup mixed with fresh lemon and/or lime juice. It's a convenient shortcut used by many bartenders; it can be found in liquor stores but is also very simple to make at home.

Amaretto Stone Sour

Apple Martini

2 ounces vodka
1 ounce apple schnapps
1 ounce apple juice
Apple slice

Fill cocktail shaker half full with ice; add vodka, apple schnapps and apple juice. Shake until blended; strain into chilled martini glass. Garnish with apple slice.

Sour Apple Martini: Substitute sour apple schnapps for apple schnapps. Garnish with Granny Smith apple slice.

Lemon Drop

Lemon wedge or slice
1 teaspoon sugar
2 ounces vodka
Juice of ½ lemon
½ ounce simple syrup*

*To make simple syrup, bring 1 cup water to a boil; stir in 1 cup sugar. Reduce heat to low; stir constantly until sugar is dissolved. Cool syrup to room temperature; store in glass jar in refrigerator.

Rub rim of chilled martini glass or shot glass with lemon wedge; dip in sugar. Fill cocktail shaker half full with ice; add vodka, lemon juice and simple syrup. Shake until blended; strain into prepared glass. Garnish with lemon wedge.

Sour Apple Martini

Fuzzy Navel

1½ ounces peach schnapps
1 ounce vodka (optional)
4 ounces orange juice
Orange wedge or slice

Fill cocktail shaker half full with ice; add peach schnapps, vodka, if desired, and orange juice. Shake until blended; strain into chilled old fashioned glass or highball glass. Garnish with orange slice.

Palmetto

1½ ounces light rum
1 ounce sweet vermouth
2 dashes orange bitters
Lemon twist

Fill cocktail shaker half full with ice; add rum, vermouth and bitters. Shake until blended; strain into chilled martini glass. Garnish with lemon twist.

The easiest way to cut a lemon twist is with citrus stripper or zester (available at kitchenware stores), which removes the peel from the fruit without the bitter white pith underneath. Or you can use a vegetable peeler or paring knife to remove thin strips of peel from the lemon. Hold both ends of the peel and twist it over the top of the drink before dropping it in—this releases a small spray of lemon oil into the cocktail.

Fuzzy Navel

Whiskey Sour

2 ounces whiskey
Juice of ½ lemon
1 teaspoon powdered sugar *or* 1 tablespoon simple syrup
Lemon or orange slice and maraschino cherry

Fill cocktail shaker half full with ice; add whiskey, lemon juice and sugar. Shake until blended; strain into ice-filled old fashioned glass. Garnish with lemon slice and maraschino cherry.

Variation: Fill cocktail shaker half full with ice; add 1½ ounces whiskey and 4 ounces sweet and sour mix. Shake until blended; strain into ice-filled old fashioned glass. Garnish with lemon slice and maraschino cherry.

Rusty Nail

1½ ounces Scotch
1 ounce Drambuie

Stir together Scotch and Drambuie in ice-filled old fashioned glass.

Drambuie is a Scottish liqueur made from aged malt whiskey, herbs, spices and heather honey. The name Drambuie is Gaelic for "the drink that satisfies."

Whiskey Sour

Singapore Sling

1 ounce gin
½ ounce cherry liqueur
¼ ounce orange liqueur
¼ ounce Bénédictine
4 ounces pineapple juice (½ cup)
½ ounce grenadine
½ ounce lime juice
Dash bitters
Pineapple wedge and maraschino cherry

Fill cocktail shaker half full with ice; add all ingredients except garnishes. Shake until blended; strain into ice-filled hurricane glass or highball glass. Garnish with maraschino cherry and pineapple.

Gin Daisy

2 ounces gin
1 ounce peach schnapps
1 ounce lemon juice
1 teaspoon grenadine
½ teaspoon powdered sugar
Cold club soda
Orange slice and maraschino cherry

Fill cocktail shaker half full with ice; add gin, schnapps, lemon juice, grenadine and sugar. Shake until blended; strain into ice-filled highball glass. Top with club soda. Garnish with orange slice and maraschino cherry.

Singapore Sling

Grasshopper

2 ounces crème de menthe
2 ounces crème de cacao
2 ounces half-and-half or whipping cream

Fill cocktail shaker half full with ice; add crème de menthe, crème de cacao and half-and-half. Shake until blended; strain into chilled martini glass.

Black Russian

2 ounces vodka
1 ounce coffee liqueur

Fill cocktail glass with ice; stir in vodka and liqueur.

White Russian: Float 1 tablespoon cream over top of Black Russian.

For the best results when bartending at home, purchase a stainless steel cocktail shaker, as the aluminum models don't get drinks as cold. Look for a standard cocktail shaker which has a lid with a built-in strainer for convenience, rather than the Boston shaker that requires a coil strainer to prevent ice from getting in your drinks.

Grasshopper

Bay Breeze

1½ ounces vodka
4 ounces pineapple juice (½ cup)
1 ounce cranberry juice

Fill martini glass or highball glass with ice; add vodka, pineapple juice and cranberry juice. Stir well.

Sea Breeze

1½ ounces vodka
3 ounces cranberry juice
2 ounces grapefruit juice
Lime wedge

Fill highball glass or martini glass with ice; add vodka, cranberry juice and grapefruit juice. Stir well. Garnish with lime wedge.

For great-tasting drinks, you need good ice. It sounds strange, but the ice you use *can* make a difference. Ice from the icemaker in your freezer may have off flavors and odors from other foods, and ice made from strongly-flavored tap water can also ruin a drink. Buying packaged ice from a supermarket or convenience store is an easy and inexpensive way to make sure your cocktails are the best they can be.

Bay Breeze

Clam Digger

1½ ounces vodka
3 ounces clam juice
3 ounces tomato juice
1 ounce lemon juice
Dash hot pepper
Dash Worcestershire sauce
Salt and black pepper
Celery stalk and lemon wedge

Fill cocktail shaker half full with ice; add vodka, clam juice, tomato juice, lemon juice, hot pepper sauce, Worcestershire, salt and pepper. Shake until blended; strain into ice-filled goblet or highball glass. Garnish with celery and lemon wedge.

Salty Dog

6 ounces grapefruit juice (¾ cup)
Salt
1½ ounces vodka

Moisten rim of highball glass with grapefruit juice; dip in salt. Fill glass with ice; pour vodka over ice. Add grapefruit juice and stir.

Greyhound: Omit salt.

Clam Digger

Long Island Iced Tea

½ ounce vodka
½ ounce light rum
½ ounce gin
½ ounce triple sec
½ ounce tequila
1 ounce lemon juice
1 teaspoon sugar or simple syrup
Cola
Lemon wedge and maraschino cherry

Fill cocktail shaker half full with ice; add vodka, rum, gin, triple sec, tequila, lemon juice and sugar. Shake until blended; strain into ice-filled highball glass. Top with cola. Garnish with lemon wedge and maraschino cherry.

Zombie

2 ounces light rum
1 ounce dark rum
½ ounce apricot brandy
1 ounce lime juice
1 ounce pineapple juice
1 ounce orange juice or papaya juice
1 teaspoon sugar
½ cup crushed ice
½ ounce 151-proof rum
½ ounce grenadine
Pineapple spear, orange slice, maraschino cherry and mint sprig

Combine light rum, dark rum, brandy, lime juice, pineapple juice, orange juice, sugar and ice in blender; blend until smooth. Pour mixture into chilled Collins glass or highball glass. Float 151-proof rum and grenadine on top. Garnish with pineapple spear, orange slice, maraschino cherry and mint sprig.

Long Island Iced Tea

Mudslide

1 ounce vodka
1 ounce Irish cream liqueur
1 ounce coffee liqueur

Fill cocktail shaker half full with ice; add vodka and liqueurs. Shake until blended; strain into chilled highball glass.

Frozen Mudslide

1 ounce vodka
1 ounce Irish cream liqueur
1 ounce coffee liqueur
1 cup vanilla ice cream
   Half-and-half (optional)
   Maraschino cherry

Combine vodka, liqueurs and ice cream in blender; blend at high speed until smooth. Add half-and-half, if desired, to reach desired consistency. Pour into chilled highball glass or margarita glass. Garnish with maraschino cherry.

Irish cream liqueurs are based on Irish whiskey and made with cream, sugar and cocoa. There are numerous brands of Irish cream liqueurs available that vary somewhat in flavor, color and texture.

Mudslides

FUN & FESTIVE

You can't celebrate Cinco de Mayo without Margaritas, and Kentucky Derby Day just wouldn't be the same without a Mint Julep. From backyard barbecues to holiday open houses, there's a perfect drink for every occasion.

White Sangria

Grog

Margarita

Lime slice
Coarse salt
2 ounces tequila
1 ounce triple sec
1 ounce lemon or lime juice

Rub rim of margarita glass with lime slice; dip in salt. Fill cocktail shaker half full with ice; add tequila, triple sec and lemon juice. Shake until blended; strain into prepared glass. Garnish with lime slice.

Frozen Margarita: Rub rim of margarita glass with lime slice; dip in coarse salt. Combine tequila, triple sec, lime juice and 1 cup ice in blender; blend until smooth. Pour into prepared glass. Garnish with lime slice.

Frozen Strawberry Margarita: Rub rim of margarita glass with lime slice; dip in coarse salt. Combine tequila, triple sec, lime juice, ½ cup frozen strawberries and ½ cup ice in blender; blend until smooth. Pour into prepared glass. Garnish with lime slice and strawberry.

Sombrero

2 ounces coffee liqueur
1 ounce cream

Fill old fashioned glass with ice; add liqueur. Pour cream over back of spoon on top of coffee liqueur. Do not stir.

Margarita

Hurricane

2 ounces light rum
2 ounces dark rum
1 ounce passion fruit juice
1 ounce orange juice
1 ounce lime juice
½ ounce grenadine
Pineapple wedge and maraschino cherry

Fill cocktail shaker half full with ice; add rum, passion fruit juice, orange juice, lime juice and grenadine. Shake until blended; strain into ice-filled hurricane glass. Garnish with pineapple wedge and maraschino cherry.

Planter's Punch

2 ounces dark rum
3 ounces orange juice
Juice of ½ lime
2 teaspoons powdered sugar
¼ teaspoon grenadine
Orange slice and maraschino cherry

Fill cocktail shaker half full with ice; add rum, orange juice, lime juice, sugar and grenadine. Shake until blended; strain into ice-filled highball glass. Garnish with orange slice and maraschino cherry.

Hurricane

Eggnog

1½ ounces brandy
¼ to ½ cup milk
1 egg
2 teaspoons simple syrup*
¼ teaspoon vanilla (optional)
Ground nutmeg

To make simple syrup, bring 1 cup water to a boil; stir in 1 cup sugar. Reduce heat to low; stir constantly until sugar is dissolved. Cool syrup to room temperature; store in glass jar in refrigerator.

Fill cocktail shaker half full with ice; add brandy, milk, egg, simple syrup, and vanilla, if desired. Shake until blended; strain into mug, highball glass or wine glass. Sprinkle with nutmeg.

Variation: Blend brandy, milk, egg, simple syrup and vanilla in blender; pour into glass. Sprinkle with nutmeg.

Oatmeal Cookie Cocktail

½ ounce butterscotch schnapps
½ ounce cinnamon schnapps
½ ounce Irish cream liqueur

Pour butterscotch schnapps into shot glass. Pour cinnamon schnapps over back of spoon on top of butterscotch schnapps. Repeat with Irish cream liqueur. Do not stir.

Tip: For successful layering of liqueurs, keep the glass still and pour very slowly and steadily over the back of the spoon—rapid pouring or stop-and-start pouring will not create the desired effect.

Eggnog

Cuba Libre

2 ounces light rum
Chilled cola
Lime wedge and/or lime slice

Fill highball glass with ice. Pour rum over ice; fill with cola. Garnish with lime wedge.

Mai Tai

1 ounce light rum
1 ounce triple sec
½ ounce grenadine
½ ounce orgeat syrup*
½ ounce lime juice
1 ounce dark rum
Pineapple wedge and maraschino cherry

*Almond-flavored syrup.

Fill cocktail shaker half full with ice; add light rum, triple sec, grenadine, orgeat syrup and lime juice. Shake until blended; strain into chilled old fashioned glass. Pour dark rum over top; do not stir. Garnish with pineapple wedge and maraschino cherry; serve with straw.

Cuba Libre

Mexican Coffee

1 ounce coffee liqueur
½ ounce tequila
¾ cup hot coffee
Whipped cream
Grated chocolate, ground nutmeg or cocoa powder

Pour liqueur and tequila into warm mug; stir in coffee. Top with whipped cream; sprinkle with grated chocolate.

Irish Coffee

6 ounces strong hot coffee
2 teaspoons brown sugar
2 ounces Irish whiskey
¼ cup whipping cream

Combine coffee and sugar in warm Irish coffee glass or mug. Stir in whiskey. Pour cream over back of spoon on top of coffee.

If you're going to be bartending frequently, you might want to purchase a jigger to make measuring easier. Jiggers come in all sizes; the most common one has a 1-ounce measure on one end and a 1½-ounce measure on the opposite end.

Mexican Coffee

Sangria

Makes 8 to 10 servings

4 medium oranges, divided
2 lemons, divided
2 bottles (750 ml each) red wine
6 ounces orange liqueur
3 ounces brandy
⅓ to ½ cup sugar
2 cups cold club soda
1 apple, diced

Juice 3 oranges and 1 lemon; pour juice into punch bowl. Add wine, liqueur, brandy and sugar; mix well to dissolve sugar. Cover and refrigerate 2 to 6 hours. Just before serving, slice or dice remaining orange and lemon. Stir club soda into sangria; add sliced orange, lemon and apple.

White Sangria

Makes 8 to 10 servings

2 oranges, cut into ¼-inch slices
2 lemons, cut into ¼-inch slices
½ cup sugar
2 bottles (750 ml each) dry, fruity white wine (such as Pinot Grigio), chilled
4 ounces peach schnapps
3 ripe peaches, pitted and cut into wedges

Place orange and lemon slices in large punch bowl. Pour sugar over fruit; mash lightly until sugar dissolves and fruit begins to break down. Stir in wine, schnapps and peaches. Refrigerate at least 2 hours or up to 10 hours.

Sangria

Champagne Cocktail

1 sugar cube
Dash bitters
Chilled champagne or dry sparkling wine
Lemon twist

Sprinkle sugar cube with bitters; place in chilled champagne flute. Fill glass with champagne; garnish with lemon twist.

Champagne Cooler

1½ ounces brandy
1 ounce triple sec
8 ounces chilled champagne

Combine brandy and triple sec in wine glass; top with champagne.

To open a bottle of champagne properly, first remove the foil and wire that is wrapped around the cork. Keep one hand (or a towel) over the cork and rotate the bottle—not the cork—with the other hand until the cork begins to loosen and you are able to remove it. There should only be a small hissing noise when the cork comes out, not a loud pop.

Champagne Cocktails

Piña Colada

1½ ounces light rum
1½ ounces cream of coconut
½ cup pineapple juice
½ cup crushed ice
Pineapple wedge and maraschino cherry

Place rum, cream of coconut and pineapple juice in blender. Add ice; blend 15 seconds or until smooth. Pour into goblet or highball glass. Garnish with pineapple wedge and maraschino cherry.

Piñita Colada: Omit rum.

Kiwi Colada: Peel, halve and seed 1 kiwi. Add to blender with ice; blend 15 seconds or until smooth. Pour into cocktail glass; garnish with kiwi slice, lemon peel and mint sprig.

Chi Chi

1½ ounces vodka
2 ounces pineapple juice
1 ounce cream of coconut
½ cup crushed ice
Pineapple wedge and maraschino cherry

Combine vodka, pineapple juice, cream of coconut and ice in blender; blend 15 seconds or until smooth. Pour into chilled Collins glass. Garnish with pineapple wedge and maraschino cherry.

Piña Colada

Tequila Sunrise

2 ounces tequila
6 ounces orange juice (¾ cup)
1 tablespoon grenadine
Orange slice and maraschino cherry

Place about 4 ice cubes in goblet or highball glass. Pour tequila and orange juice over ice; do not stir. Pour in grenadine and let sink to bottom of glass; do not stir. Garnish with orange slice and maraschino cherry.

Mint Julep

4 to 6 fresh mint leaves
1 teaspoon sugar
3 ounces bourbon
Fresh mint sprig

Combine mint leaves and sugar in Collins glass or highball glass. Fill glass with ice; pour in bourbon. Garnish with mint sprig.

The traditional container for a mint julep is a silver julep cup or mug, but a Collins glass is more commonly used. For strong flavor, the mint should be mashed with the sugar in the bottom of the glass to release its flavor. Professional bartenders and connoisseurs use a muddler (a wooden rod with one wide end similar to a pestle) to crush the mint, but it can also be done with the back of a spoon.

Tequila Sunrise

Electric Lemonade

1½ ounces vodka
½ ounce blue curaçao
2 ounces sweet and sour mix
Lemon-lime soda
Lime wedges

Fill Collins glass half full with ice; add vodka, curaçao and sour mix. Fill with lemon-lime soda. Garnish with lime wedges.

Blue Hawaiian

1 ounce light rum
½ ounce blue curaçao
1 ounce pineapple juice
1 ounce cream of coconut
1 teaspoon sugar
Strawberry and pineapple slice

Fill cocktail shaker half full with ice; add rum, curaçao, pineapple juice, cream of coconut and sugar. Shake until blended; strain into ice-filled old fashioned glass. Garnish with strawberry and pineapple slice.

Note: Curaçao is the name for liqueur flavored from the dried peel of bitter oranges grown on the Caribbean island of Curaçao. The liqueur is naturally colorless, but some varieties are amber and some are tinted blue or other colors.

Electric Lemonade

Hot Toddy

Lemon wedge
1 teaspoon honey or sugar
¾ cup hot brewed tea or hot water
1½ ounces whiskey or brandy
Cinnamon stick

Squeeze lemon wedge into warm mug or Irish coffee glass; stir in honey and drop lemon into mug. Stir in hot tea and whiskey with cinnamon stick.

Grog

2 ounces dark rum
½ ounce lemon juice
1 teaspoon brown sugar or granulated sugar
2 to 3 whole cloves
¾ cup hot water
1 cinnamon stick

Combine rum, lemon juice, sugar and cloves in warm mug. Stir in hot water with cinnamon stick until sugar is dissolved.

Hot Buttered Rum

1 teaspoon brown sugar
¾ to 1 cup hot water or milk
2 ounces rum
2 teaspoons butter
Ground nutmeg

Place sugar in warm Irish coffee glass or mug; stir in hot water. Stir in rum. Float butter on top and sprinkle with nutmeg.

Hot Toddy

Frozen Daiquiri

1½ ounces light rum
½ ounce triple sec
1½ ounces lime juice (about 1 lime)
1 teaspoon powdered sugar or simple syrup
1 cup crushed ice
Lime slice

Place rum, triple sec, lime juice and sugar in blender. Add ice; blend 15 seconds or until smooth. Pour into goblet or margarita glass; garnish with lime slice.

Frozen Strawberry Daiquiri: Add 4 to 5 chopped strawberries and ¼ ounce strawberry liqueur to blender with ice. Garnish with strawberry and lime twist.

Daiquiri

1½ ounces light rum
¾ ounce lime juice
1 teaspoon simple syrup* or powdered sugar
Lime slice

*To make simple syrup, bring 1 cup water to a boil; stir in 1 cup sugar. Reduce heat to low; stir constantly until sugar is dissolved. Cool syrup to room temperature; store in glass jar in refrigerator.

Fill cocktail shaker half full with ice; add rum, lime juice and simple syrup. Shake until blended; strain into chilled martini glass or margarita glass. Garnish with lime slice.

Frozen Strawberry Daiquiri

COOL PARTY FOOD

*C*ocktails are best enjoyed with a few savory snacks—simple nibbles like Paprika-Spiced Almonds and Citrus-Marinated Olives, or more elegant fare such as Pesto Terrine and Roast Beef Roll-Ups.

Mojito Shrimp Cocktail

Onion & White Bean Spread

Chickpea, Roasted Pepper & Olive Toasts

Makes 24 appetizers

> 2 cloves garlic, peeled
> 1 can (about 15 ounces) chickpeas, rinsed and drained
> 1 cup drained chopped roasted red peppers
> ¼ cup olive oil
>   Salt and black pepper
> ½ cup drained pitted black olives
> ½ cup drained pimiento-stuffed green olives
> 24 (½-inch) toasted French bread slices

1. Add garlic to food processor with motor running. Add chickpeas and red peppers; process until paste forms. Add oil; process until smooth. Transfer chickpea mixture to medium bowl; season with salt and pepper. Cover and let stand 30 minutes.

2. Place black and green olives in clean food processor. Process with on/off pulses until olives are coarsely chopped.

3. Spread 2 tablespoons chickpea mixture on each bread slice. Spoon 1 tablespoon olive mixture in center of chickpea mixture. Serve at room temperature.

Roast Beef Roll-Ups

Makes 12 appetizers

> 1 package (8 ounces) cream cheese, softened
> 1 cup (4 ounces) crumbled blue cheese
> 1 teaspoon Dijon mustard
> ½ teaspoon black pepper
> 1 pound sliced deli roast beef
> 1 small red onion, thinly sliced
> 12 butter lettuce leaves (about 1 head)

1. Mix cream cheese, blue cheese, mustard and pepper in small bowl until well blended.

2. Spread each slice of roast beef with 1 tablespoon cheese mixture. Top with 1 to 2 slices onion and 1 leaf lettuce. Roll up roast beef slices starting at short end; secure with toothpicks, if necessary. Arrange rolls on serving platter. Cover and refrigerate until ready to serve.

Chickpea, Roasted Pepper & Olive Toasts

Szechwan Chicken Cucumber Cups

Makes 20 appetizers

1½ cups finely shredded or chopped skinless rotisserie chicken
1 tablespoon rice vinegar
1 tablespoon soy sauce
1½ teaspoons dark sesame oil
1 teaspoon grated fresh ginger
⅛ teaspoon red pepper flakes
1 large seedless cucumber (about 1 pound)
¼ cup chopped fresh cilantro

1. Combine chicken, vinegar, soy sauce, sesame oil, ginger and red pepper flakes in medium bowl; mix well.

2. Trim off ends of cucumber. Use fork to score all sides of cucumber lengthwise (or peel cucumber lengthwise in alternating strips). Cut crosswise into 20 (½-inch) slices. Use melon baller or grapefruit spoon to scoop out indentation in one cut side of each slice to form cup.

3. Mound 1 tablespoon chicken mixture in each cup. Sprinkle with cilantro. Serve immediately or cover and refrigerate up to 2 hours before serving.

Onion & White Bean Spread

Makes 1¼ cups

1 can (about 15 ounces) cannellini or Great Northern beans, rinsed and drained
¼ cup chopped green onions
¼ cup grated Parmesan cheese
¼ cup olive oil
1 tablespoon fresh rosemary, chopped
2 cloves garlic, minced
Additional olive oil
French bread slices

1. Combine beans, green onions, Parmesan, oil, rosemary and garlic in food processor; process 30 to 40 seconds or until almost smooth.

2. Spoon bean mixture into serving bowl. Drizzle additional olive oil over spread just before serving. Serve with bread.

Szechwan Chicken Cucumber Cups

Paprika-Spiced Almonds

Makes 1 cup

1 cup whole blanched almonds
1 teaspoon olive oil
¼ teaspoon coarse salt
¼ teaspoon smoked paprika or paprika

1. Preheat oven to 375°F. Spread almonds in single layer in shallow baking pan. Bake 8 to 10 minutes or until almonds are lightly browned. Transfer to bowl; cool 5 to 10 minutes.

2. Toss almonds with oil until completely coated. Sprinkle with salt and paprika; toss again.

Tip: For the best flavor, serve these almonds the day they are made.

Mojito Shrimp Cocktail

Makes 6 to 8 servings

1 pound medium frozen raw shrimp, deveined but not peeled
1 cup plus 2 tablespoons prepared mojito cocktail mix, divided
2 tablespoons olive oil
1 jar shrimp cocktail sauce

1. Place shrimp in large shallow glass dish. Pour 1 cup mojito mix over shrimp to cover. (Separate shrimp as much as possible to aid thawing.) Marinate in refrigerator 10 to 24 hours, stirring shrimp once or twice until thawed.

2. Prepare grill for direct cooking. Drain shrimp; discard marinade. *Do not peel.* Pat dry and place in large bowl with oil; toss to coat.

3. Grill over medium high heat on grill topper* 10 to 15 minutes or until shrimp are pink and opaque, turning once. Refrigerate until ready to serve.

4. Pour cocktail sauce into serving bowl; stir in remaining 1 to 2 tablespoons mojito mix. Peel shrimp before serving or provide bowl for shells.

*Shrimp may also be cooked in grill pan.

Variation: Add fresh chopped mint to cocktail sauce instead of, or in addition to, mojito mix. Serve with lime wedges.

Paprika-Spiced Almonds

Rosemary Wine Crackers

Makes about 24 crackers

1 cup whole wheat flour
1 tablespoon chopped fresh rosemary leaves
⅛ teaspoon salt
3 tablespoons olive oil
¼ cup wine (preferably a fruity white or rosé)
Coarse salt (optional)

1. Preheat oven to 400°F. Line large cookie sheet with parchment paper; sprinkle paper lightly with flour.

2. Place flour, rosemary and salt in food processor; process with on/off pulses 30 seconds to combine. With motor running, add olive oil and wine gradually through feed tube. Stop adding wine when mixture forms a ball of dough on top of blade. Remove dough to prepared cookie sheet.

3. Roll dough as thin as possible (⅛ inch or less) on cookie sheet. Sprinkle with coarse salt, if desired, and roll lightly to press salt into dough. Score crackers into squares or diamonds with knife or pizza cutter .

4. Bake 10 to 15 minutes or until crackers begin to brown around edges, rotating cookie sheet halfway through baking time. Remove to wire rack to cool. Break into individual crackers. Store in airtight container. To re-crisp, place crackers in 350°F oven for 5 minutes.

Note: Making crackers is surprisingly easy. This recipe can easily be doubled or adjusted to suit personal tastes. Because crackers don't need to rise, whole wheat flour works well. You could also swap out some of the wheat flour for rye or buckwheat flour. Instead of wine, you could use fruit juice or even water.

Rosemary Wine Crackers

Citrus-Marinated Olives

Makes 2 cups

> 1 cup (about 8 ounces) large green olives, drained
> 1 cup kalamata olives, rinsed and drained
> 1/3 cup extra virgin olive oil
> 1/4 cup orange juice
> 3 tablespoons sherry vinegar or red wine vinegar
> 2 tablespoons lemon juice
> 1 tablespoon grated orange peel
> 1 tablespoon grated lemon peel
> 1/2 teaspoon ground cumin
> 1/4 teaspoon red pepper flakes

Combine all ingredients in medium glass bowl. Let stand overnight at room temperature; refrigerate for up to two weeks.

Spanish Ham & Cheese Toasts

Makes 24 appetizers

> 1/2 (11-ounce) package goat cheese, at room temperature
> 1 teaspoon ground cumin
> 1/2 teaspoon smoked paprika or paprika
> 24 (1/2-inch) toasted French bread slices
> 1/2 cup chopped fresh parsley
> 8 slices Serrano ham or prosciutto, cut crosswise into thirds

1. Place goat cheese in small bowl. Add cumin and paprika; stir until well blended and uniform in color. Cover and let stand 30 minutes.

2. Spread goat cheese mixture on bread slices; sprinkle with parsley. Top each toast with 1 piece ham. Serve at room temperature.

Tip: The goat cheese mixture can be prepared up to 2 days in advance. This will allow plenty of time for the flavors to blend. For the best flavor, remove the goat cheese mixture from the refrigerator 30 minutes before assembling the toasts.

Citrus-Marinated Olives

Pesto Terrine

Makes 6 to 8 servings

 1 package (8 ounces) cream cheese, softened, divided
 2 tablespoons butter, softened, divided
 5 tablespoons basil pesto, divided
 ¼ cup sun-dried tomato pesto
 Assorted crackers or toasts

1. Line 1- to 1½-cup bowl or mold with plastic wrap. Allow edges of wrap to extend over sides of bowl.

2. Place half of cream cheese, 1 tablespoon butter and 4 tablespoons basil pesto in food processor. Process with on/off pulses until well blended, scraping down side of bowl frequently. Transfer mixture to prepared bowl; press down firmly. Gently spread remaining 1 tablespoon basil pesto on top of mixture. (Drain as much oil as possible from pesto before spreading.)

3. Place remaining half of cream cheese, 1 tablespoon butter and sun-dried tomato pesto in clean food processor. Process with on/off pulses until well blended. Spread mixture over basil pesto and press down firmly, smoothing top. Cover and refrigerate terrine at least 1 hour.

4. To serve, place small plate on top of bowl and invert; remove bowl and plastic wrap. Smooth surface with knife and blot excess oil with paper towel. Serve terrine with crackers or toasts.

Serving Suggestion: Top the terrine with chopped sun-dried tomatoes. Garnish with fresh basil.

Quick Roasted Red Pepper Dip

Makes about 2 cups

 2 cups crumbled feta cheese
 2 tablespoons garlic olive oil
 ¼ teaspoon black pepper
 1 cup roasted red peppers
 Pita chips or vegetable dippers

1. Place feta, oil and black pepper in food processor; process 1 minute or until smooth.

2. Add red peppers; process 10 to 15 seconds until blended but not puréed. Serve with pita chips or vegetable dippers.

Pesto Terrine

Marinated Antipasto

Makes about 5 cups

- ¼ **cup extra virgin olive oil**
- 2 **tablespoons balsamic vinegar**
- 1 **clove garlic, minced**
- ½ **teaspoon sugar**
- ½ **teaspoon salt**
- ¼ **teaspoon black pepper**
- 1 **pint (2 cups) cherry tomatoes**
- 1 **can (14 ounces) quartered artichoke hearts, drained**
- 8 **ounces small balls or cubes fresh mozzarella cheese**
- 1 **cup drained pitted kalamata olives**
- ¼ **cup sliced fresh basil leaves**
- **Lettuce leaves**

1. Whisk oil, vinegar, garlic, sugar, salt and pepper in medium bowl. Add tomatoes, artichokes, mozzarella, olives and basil; toss to coat. Let stand at room temperature 30 minutes.

2. Line platter with lettuce. Arrange antipasto over lettuce.

Serving Suggestion: Serve antipasto with toothpicks as an appetizer or spoon over Bibb lettuce leaves for a first-course salad.

Kalamata olives may be purchased already pitted, or you can save money and remove the pits yourself. One method of pitting an olive is to place the flat side of a chef's knife over the olive and pound on it with a clenched fist. The pit may pop out or be easily squeezed out with your fingers.

Marinated Antipasto

Chorizo & Caramelized Onion Tortilla

Makes 36 appetizers

¼ **cup olive oil**
3 **medium yellow onions, quartered and sliced**
½ **pound Spanish chorizo (about 2 links) or andouille sausage, diced**
6 **eggs**
   Salt and black pepper
½ **cup chopped fresh parsley**

1. Preheat oven to 350°F. Spray 9-inch square baking pan with olive oil cooking spray.

2. Heat oil in medium skillet over medium heat. Add onions; cook, covered, 10 minutes or until onions are translucent. Reduce heat to low; cook, uncovered, 40 minutes or until golden and very tender. Remove onions from skillet; set aside to cool.

3. Add chorizo to same skillet. Cook over medium heat, stirring occasionally, 5 minutes or until chorizo just begins to brown. Remove from skillet; set aside to cool.

4. Whisk eggs in medium bowl; season with salt and pepper. Add onions, chorizo and parsley; stir gently until well blended. Pour egg mixture into prepared pan.

5. Bake 12 to 15 minutes or until center is almost set. *Turn oven to broil.* Broil 1 to 2 minutes or until top just begins to brown. Remove pan to wire rack; cool completely. Cut into 36 squares; serve cold or at room temperature.

Tip: The tortilla can be made up to 1 day ahead and refrigerated until ready to serve. To serve at room temperature, remove the tortilla from the refrigerator 30 minutes before serving.

Chorizo & Caramelized Onion Tortilla

Elegant Appetizer Bites

Makes 30 appetizers

1 package (8 ounces) cream cheese, softened
2 ounces feta cheese with basil and tomato or plain feta
2 cloves garlic, minced
30 mini phyllo shells (two 2.1-ounce packages) *or* 15 mini puff pastry
   shells
Prepared toppings such as sundried tomato pesto, red pepper and
   artichoke tapenade, basil pesto and/or black olive spread

1. Beat cream cheese, feta and garlic in small bowl with electric mixer at low speed until well blended.

2. Spoon about 1½ teaspoons cheese mixture into each shell. Top with ½ teaspoon desired topping.

Smoked Salmon Dip

Makes 1³/₄ cups dip

4 ounces smoked salmon
1 container (8 ounces) whipped cream cheese
½ cup finely chopped tomatoes
¼ cup minced green onions (green part only)
2 teaspoons capers
Unsalted pretzel crackers

1. Finely chop salmon or process in food processor until minced.

2. Place salmon in medium bowl. Stir in cream cheese, tomatoes, green onions and capers; mix well. Serve with pretzel crackers.

Notes: Don't use top-quality smoked salmon in this recipe; less expensive salmon works well. The dip can be prepared one day in advance, covered with plastic wrap and refrigerated.

Elegant Appetizer Bites

Chili Cashews

Makes 2 cups

> 1 tablespoon vegetable oil
> 2 teaspoons chili powder
> 1 teaspoon ground cumin
> ½ teaspoon sugar
> ½ teaspoon red pepper flakes
> 2 cups roasted salted whole cashews (about 9 ounces)

1. Preheat oven to 350°F. Line baking sheet with foil; spray foil with nonstick cooking spray.

2. Combine oil, chili powder, cumin, sugar and red pepper flakes in medium bowl; stir until well blended. Add cashews, stirring to coat evenly. Spread cashews in single layer on prepared baking sheet.

3. Bake 8 to 10 minutes or until golden, stirring once. Cool completely on baking sheet. Store in airtight container.

Edamame Hummus

Makes about 2 cups

> 1 package (16 ounces) frozen shelled edamame, thawed
> 2 green onions, coarsely chopped
> ½ cup loosely packed fresh cilantro
> 3 to 4 tablespoons water
> 2 tablespoons canola oil
> 1½ tablespoons fresh lime juice
> 1 tablespoon honey
> 2 cloves garlic
> 1 teaspoon salt
> ¼ teaspoon black pepper
>   Rice crackers, baby carrots, cucumber slices and sugar snap peas

1. Combine edamame, green onions, cilantro, 3 tablespoons water, oil, lime juice, honey, garlic, salt and pepper in food processor; process until smooth. Add additional water to thin dip, if necessary.

2. Serve with crackers and vegetables for dipping. Store leftover dip in refrigerator up to 4 days.

Chili Cashews

Artichoke Cheese Toasts

Makes 24 appetizers

  1 jar (8 ounces) marinated artichoke hearts, drained
  ½ cup (2 ounces) shredded Swiss cheese
  ⅓ cup finely chopped roasted red peppers
  ⅓ cup finely chopped celery
  2 tablespoons mayonnaise
24 melba toast rounds
    Paprika (optional)

1. Preheat broiler. Rinse artichokes under cold running water; drain well. Pat dry with paper towels. Finely chop artichokes; place in medium bowl. Add cheese, red peppers, celery and mayonnaise; mix well.

2. Spoon artichoke mixture evenly onto melba toast rounds; place on large baking sheet or broiler pan. Broil 6 inches from heat 45 seconds or until cheese mixture is bubbly and heated through. Sprinkle with paprika, if desired.

Olive Tapenade

Makes 1¾ cups

1 can (16 ounces) medium pitted black olives
½ cup pimiento-stuffed green olives
1 tablespoon roasted garlic*
½ teaspoon dry mustard
½ cup (2 ounces) crumbled feta cheese
1 tablespoon olive oil
   Toasted French bread slices

To roast garlic, preheat oven to 400°F. Remove outer layers of papery skin and cut ¼ inch off top of garlic head. Place cut side up on piece of heavy-duty foil. Drizzle with olive oil; wrap tightly in foil. Bake 25 to 30 minutes or until cloves are soft. Cool slightly; squeeze out garlic pulp.

1. Combine olives, roasted garlic and mustard in food processor or blender; process until finely chopped.

2. Combine olive mixture, feta and oil in medium bowl; stir until well blended. Serve with toasted bread slices.

Tip: For the best flavor, prepare the tapenade several hours or one day ahead to allow the flavors to blend.

Artichoke Cheese Toasts

Smoked Salmon Omelet Roll-Ups

Makes about 24 appetizers

    4 eggs
    ⅛ teaspoon black pepper
    ¼ cup chive and onion cream cheese, softened
    1 package (about 4 ounces) smoked salmon, cut into bite-size pieces

1. Beat eggs and pepper in small bowl until well blended (no streaks of white showing). Spray large nonstick skillet with nonstick cooking spray; heat over medium-high heat.

2. Pour half of egg mixture into skillet; tilt skillet to completely coat bottom with thin layer of eggs. Cook, without stirring, 2 to 4 minutes or until eggs are set. Use spatula to carefully loosen omelet from skillet; slide onto cutting board. Repeat with remaining egg mixture to make second omelet.

3. Spread 2 tablespoons cream cheese over each omelet; top with smoked salmon. Roll up omelets tightly; wrap in plastic wrap and refrigerate at least 30 minutes. Cut off ends, then cut rolls crosswise into ½-inch slices.

Marinated Mushrooms

Makes 4 to 6 servings

    3 tablespoons olive oil, divided
    8 ounces cremini mushrooms, halved
    1 clove garlic, crushed
    ½ cup chicken or vegetable broth
    1 teaspoon lemon juice
    Salt and black pepper

1. Heat 2 tablespoons oil in large skillet over medium-high heat. Add mushrooms and garlic; cook and stir 5 to 6 minutes. Add broth; cook about 5 minutes or until almost all liquid evaporates. Remove from heat; cool. Discard garlic.

2. Spoon mushroom mixture into medium bowl. Stir in remaining 1 tablespoon oil and lemon juice. Season with salt and pepper. Let stand 10 minutes to blend flavors.

Note: Cremini mushrooms, sometimes called baby bella mushrooms, are small portobello mushrooms. If they are unavailable, substitute white button mushrooms.

Smoked Salmon Omelet Roll-Ups

THE HEAT IS ON

𝒟electable and diminutive, hot hors d'oeuvres are the perfect accompaniment to cool cocktails. Try Ham & Swiss Twists, Toasted Ravioli or Tiny Shrimp Tacos— they'll make your next party unforgettably delicious!

Tiny Shrimp Tacos with Peach Salsa

Mini Dizzy Dogs

Beef Empanadas

Makes 9 appetizers

1 tablespoon olive oil
3 tablespoons finely chopped onion
1 clove garlic, minced
¼ pound ground beef
2 tablespoons chopped pimiento-stuffed green olives
2 tablespoons raisins
2 tablespoons ketchup
1 tablespoon chopped fresh parsley
½ teaspoon ground cumin
1 sheet frozen puff pastry, thawed (half of 17¼-ounce package)
1 egg yolk

1. Preheat oven to 400°F. Line baking sheet with parchment paper.

2. Heat oil in large skillet over medium-high heat. Add onion and garlic; cook and stir 2 to 3 minutes. Add beef; cook 6 to 8 minutes or until browned, stirring to break up meat. Drain fat. Add olives, raisins, ketchup, parsley and cumin; cook and stir 1 to 2 minutes.

3. Roll out pastry sheet on lightly floured surface into 12-inch square. Cut into nine 4-inch squares. Place rounded tablespoonful beef mixture in center of each square. Fold over to form triangle; seal edges with fork. Place on prepared baking sheet.

4. Bake 18 to 20 minutes or until golden brown. Serve warm.

Bacon-Wrapped Dates

Makes 8 to 10 servings

1 container (12 ounces) whole Medjool dates
1 pound thick-cut bacon (about 11 slices)

1. Preheat oven to 450°F. Line shallow baking pan with parchment paper. To remove pits from dates, cut tips off each end of date. Insert flat end of wooden skewer into each date and push out pit.

2. Cut bacon slices lengthwise into halves. Wrap each date with half slice of bacon; secure bacon with toothpick. Arrange dates 1 inch apart in prepared baking pan.

3. Bake 18 to 20 minutes or until bacon is cooked, turning after 10 minutes. Remove toothpicks before serving.

Beef Empanadas

Italian Chicken Nuggets

Makes 4 to 6 servings

- ¼ cup all-purpose flour
- 1 egg, lightly beaten
- 1 cup dry bread crumbs, toasted
- ½ cup grated Parmesan cheese
- 2 teaspoons dried Italian seasoning
  - Salt and black pepper
- 3 boneless skinless chicken breasts, cut into 1-inch pieces
  - Pasta sauce, heated

1. Preheat oven to 400°F. Line baking sheet with parchment paper.

2. Place flour in shallow bowl. Place egg in second shallow bowl. Combine bread crumbs, Parmesan, Italian seasoning, salt and pepper in third shallow bowl.

3. Dip each piece of chicken into flour, then egg, then roll in bread crumb mixture. Place on prepared baking sheet. Spray chicken with olive oil nonstick cooking spray.

4. Bake about 25 minutes or until chicken is cooked through and coating is browned. Serve with pasta sauce for dipping.

Goat Cheese-Stuffed Figs

Makes 14 appetizers

- 7 fresh firm ripe figs
- 7 slices prosciutto
- 1 package (4 ounces) goat cheese
  - Ground black pepper

1. Preheat broiler. Line small baking sheet or broiler pan with foil. Cut figs in half vertically. Cut prosciutto slices in half to create 14 pieces (about 4 inches long and 1 inch wide).

2. Spread 1 teaspoon goat cheese onto cut side of each fig half. Wrap prosciutto slice around fig and goat cheese. Sprinkle with pepper.

3. Broil about 4 minutes or until cheese softens and figs are heated through.

Italian Chicken Nuggets

Mini Carnitas Tacos

Makes 36 mini tacos

1½ pounds boneless pork loin, cut into 1-inch cubes
1 onion, finely chopped
½ cup chicken broth
1 tablespoon chili powder
2 teaspoons ground cumin
1 teaspoon dried oregano
½ teaspoon minced chipotle chile in adobo sauce (optional)
½ cup pico de gallo
2 tablespoons chopped fresh cilantro
½ teaspoon salt
12 (6-inch) corn tortillas
¾ cup (3 ounces) shredded sharp Cheddar cheese
3 tablespoons sour cream

SLOW COOKER DIRECTIONS

1. Combine pork, onion, broth, chili powder, cumin, oregano and chipotle chile, if desired, in slow cooker. Cover; cook on LOW 6 hours or on HIGH 3 hours or until pork is very tender. Pour off excess cooking liquid.

2. Shred pork with 2 forks; stir in pico de gallo, cilantro and salt. Cover and keep warm.

3. Cut 3 circles from each tortilla with 2-inch biscuit cutter. Top tortillas with pork, cheese and sour cream.

Tip: Carnitas means "little meats" in Spanish. This dish is usually made with an inexpensive cut of pork that is simmered for a long time until it falls to pieces. The meat is then browned in pork fat. The slow cooker makes the long, slow cooking process easy to manage, and skipping the final browning lowers the fat content.

Mini Carnitas Tacos

Ham & Swiss Twists

Makes about 22 appetizers

> 1 package (about 13 ounces) refrigerated pizza dough
> 6 very thin slices Swiss cheese
> 6 very thin slices smoked ham
>   Black pepper

1. Preheat oven to 400°F. Line baking sheets with parchment paper.

2. Unroll dough on cutting board; press into 16×12-inch rectangle. Arrange single layer of cheese slices over half of dough, cutting slices to fit as necessary. Top with ham slices; sprinkle with pepper. Fold remaining half of dough over ham and cheese layers, creating 12×8-inch rectangle.

3. Cut dough into ½-inch strips (8 inches long). Twist strips several times; place on prepared baking sheets. Bake about 14 minutes or until golden brown. Serve warm.

Note: Ham & Swiss Twists are about 12 inches long. For smaller twists, cut them in half after baking.

Prosciutto-Wrapped Asparagus

Makes 16 appetizers

> 2 tablespoons olive oil, divided
> 16 medium asparagus spears, trimmed
> 4 ounces prosciutto, cut lengthwise into 3 strips
>   Black pepper (optional)
> ¾ cup mayonnaise
> 1 teaspoon lemon juice
> 1 clove garlic, minced

1. Preheat oven to 400°F. Brush large shallow baking pan with 1 tablespoon olive oil. Wrap each asparagus spear with 1 strip prosciutto. Place asparagus on prepared baking sheet. Brush with remaining olive oil; sprinkle with pepper, if desired.

2. Bake about 12 minutes or until asparagus is tender. Cool slightly.

3. Meanwhile, combine mayonnaise, lemon juice and garlic in small bowl until well blended. Serve asparagus warm with garlic mayonnaise.

Ham & Swiss Twists

Apricot Brie en Croûte

Makes 6 servings

1 sheet frozen puff pastry, thawed (half of 17¼-ounce package)
1 round (8 ounces) Brie cheese
¼ cup apricot preserves

1. Unfold pastry sheet on lightly floured surface. Preheat oven to 400°F. Line baking sheet with parchment paper.

2. Roll out pastry sheet into 12-inch square. Place Brie in center of square; spread preserves over top of Brie.

3. Gather up edges of puff pastry and bring together over center of Brie, covering cheese entirely. Pinch and twist pastry edges together to seal. Transfer to prepared baking sheet.

4. Bake 20 to 25 minutes or until golden brown. (If top of pastry browns too quickly, cover loosely with small piece of foil.) Serve warm.

Variation: For added flavor and texture, sprinkle 2 tablespoons sliced almonds over the preserves. Proceed with wrapping and baking the Brie as directed above.

Speedy Salami Spirals

Makes about 28 spirals

1 package (about 13 ounces) refrigerated pizza dough
1 cup (4 ounces) shredded Italian cheese blend
3 to 4 ounces thinly sliced Genoa salami

1. Preheat oven to 400°F. Line large baking sheet with parchment paper or spray with nonstick cooking spray.

2. Unroll dough on cutting board or clean work surface; press into 15×10-inch rectangle. Sprinkle evenly with cheese; top with salami.

3. Starting with long side, tightly roll up dough and filling jelly-roll style, pinching seam to seal. Cut roll crosswise into ½-inch slices; arrange slices cut side down on prepared baking sheet. (If roll is too soft to cut, refrigerate or freeze until firm.)

4. Bake about 15 minutes or until golden brown. Serve warm.

Apricot Brie en Croûte

Prosciutto-Wrapped Figs with Orange-Honey Sauce

Makes 16 appetizers

16 dried Mission figs
 8 slices prosciutto, at room temperature
 6 tablespoons orange juice
 1 tablespoon honey
 2 teaspoons lemon juice
   Red pepper flakes
   Salt (optional)

1. Place figs in small saucepan; cover with water. Bring to a boil over medium-high heat. Reduce heat; cover and simmer 8 minutes or until figs are soft. Drain and set aside to cool.

2. Meanwhile, cut prosciutto slices in half lengthwise. Wrap each fig with prosciutto strip; secure with toothpick. Arrange on serving plate.

3. Combine orange juice, honey, lemon juice, red pepper flakes and salt, if desired, in small saucepan. Bring to a boil over medium-high heat. Cook 2 minutes or until mixture is syrupy and reduced by half. Drizzle sauce over figs or serve on the side for dipping.

Mini Dizzy Dogs

Makes 20 appetizers

½ sheet refrigerated crescent roll dough (half of 8-ounce can)
20 mini hot dogs or smoked sausages
   Ketchup and mustard

1. Preheat oven to 375°F. Line baking sheet with parchment paper.

2. Cut dough into 20 (¼-inch) strips. Wrap 1 strip dough diagonally around each hot dog. Place on prepared baking sheet.

3. Bake 10 to 12 minutes or until light golden brown. Serve with ketchup and mustard for dipping.

Prosciutto-Wrapped Figs with Orange-Honey Sauce

Spicy Almond Chicken Wings

Makes about 36 appetizers

3 pounds chicken drummettes
3 tablespoons vegetable oil
2 tablespoons jerk seasoning
½ teaspoon salt
1 cup slivered almonds, finely chopped

1. Place drummettes in large bowl. Add oil, jerk seasoning and salt; toss to coat. Cover and refrigerate 20 to 30 minutes.

2. Preheat oven to 400°F. Line large baking sheet with foil. Spray with nonstick cooking spray.

3. Place almonds in shallow bowl. Roll drummettes in almonds until coated. Place on prepared baking sheet. Bake 30 to 35 minutes or until chicken is cooked through.

Mac & Cheese Mini Cups

Makes 36 appetizers

3 tablespoons butter, divided
2 tablespoons all-purpose flour
1 cup milk
1 teaspoon salt
½ teaspoon black pepper
1 cup (4 ounces) shredded sharp Cheddar cheese
1 cup (4 ounces) shredded Muenster cheese
½ pound uncooked elbow macaroni, cooked and drained
⅓ cup bread crumbs, toasted

1. Preheat oven to 400°F. Melt 1 tablespoon butter; grease 36 mini (1¾-inch) muffin pan cups with melted butter.

2. Melt remaining 2 tablespoons butter in large saucepan over medium heat. Whisk in flour; cook and stir 2 minutes. Add milk, salt and pepper; cook and stir 3 minutes or until mixture is thickened. Remove from heat; stir in cheeses. Fold in macaroni. Divide mixture among prepared muffin cups; sprinkle with bread crumbs.

3. Bake 20 to 25 minutes or until golden brown. Cool in pans 10 minutes; remove carefully using sharp knife.

Spicy Almond Chicken Wings

Grilled Cheese Kabobs

Makes 12 servings

8 thick slices whole wheat bread
3 thick slices sharp Cheddar cheese
3 thick slices Monterey Jack or Colby Jack cheese
2 tablespoons butter, melted

1. Cut each slice of bread into 1-inch squares. Cut each slice of cheese into 1-inch squares. Make small sandwiches with 1 square of bread and 1 square of each type of cheese. Top with second square of bread.

2. Place sandwiches on ends of short wooden skewers. Brush all sides of sandwiches with melted butter.

3. Heat nonstick grill pan over medium-high heat. Grill sandwich kabobs 30 seconds on each of 4 sides or until golden and cheese is slightly melted.

Toasted Ravioli

Makes 8 servings

1 package (about 9 ounces) refrigerated cheese ravioli
½ cup plain dry bread crumbs
¼ cup grated Parmesan cheese
1 teaspoon dried basil
1 teaspoon dried oregano
¼ teaspoon black pepper
2 egg whites
Spicy pasta sauce, heated, or salsa

1. Cook ravioli according to package directions. Rinse under cold running water until cool; drain well.

2. Preheat oven to 375°F. Spray baking sheet with nonstick cooking spray. Combine bread crumbs, Parmesan, basil, oregano and pepper in medium bowl.

3. Beat egg whites lightly in shallow dish. Add ravioli; toss gently to coat. Transfer ravioli, a few at a time, to bread crumb mixture; toss to coat evenly. Arrange in single layer on prepared baking sheet. Spray tops of ravioli with cooking spray.

4. Bake 12 to 14 minutes or until crisp. Serve with pasta sauce for dipping.

Grilled Cheese Kabobs

Caprese Tarts

Makes 6 tarts

3 tomatoes
3 tablespoons pesto
1 sheet frozen puff pastry, thawed (half of 17¼-ounce package)
1 ball (8 ounces) fresh mozzarella cheese
2 tablespoons kalamata olive tapenade (see Note)

1. Preheat oven to 425°F. Line baking sheet with parchment paper.

2. Cut each tomato into 4 slices about ⅓ inch thick. Discard tops and bottoms. Place in resealable food storage bag with pesto; toss to coat. Refrigerate 30 minutes.

3. Cut out 6 (4-inch) rounds from pastry sheet. Place rounds on prepared baking sheet. Top each round with 2 tomato slices. Bake 12 minutes or until pastry is puffed and light brown.

4. *Turn oven to broil.* Cut mozzarella into 6 slices. Top each tart with 1 cheese slice. Broil 1 minute or until cheese is melted. Sprinkle evenly with tapenade. Serve warm.

Note: Tapenade is a Provençal condiment made from minced olives, anchovies, capers, olive oil and seasonings. It is available in large supermarkets and specialty food stores.

The best way to thaw puff pastry is in the refrigerator. If you don't need the entire package, remove only what you need, wrap the unused portion in plastic wrap or foil and return it to the freezer. A sheet of puff pastry will thaw in about 4 hours in the refrigerator and can be held up to 2 days.

Caprese Tarts

Brie Bites

Makes 32 appetizers

> **1 package (17¼ ounces) frozen puff pastry, thawed**
> **¼ cup apricot preserves or red pepper jelly**
> **1 round (5 ounces) Brie cheese, cut into 32 chunks**

1. Preheat oven to 400°F. Cut each pastry sheet into 16 squares.

2. Spread ½ teaspoon apricot preserves on each square. Place 1 piece of Brie on one side of each square. Fold over opposite edge; use fork to seal edges completely. Place 1 inch apart on ungreased baking sheets.

3. Bake 10 to 13 minutes or until golden brown.

Tiny Shrimp Tacos with Peach Salsa

Makes 24 appetizers

> **1 peach, peeled and finely diced**
> **2 tablespoons finely chopped red onion**
> **1 small jalapeño pepper, finely chopped**
> **Juice of 1 lime**
> **1 tablespoon chopped fresh parsley or cilantro**
> **1 clove garlic, minced**
> **½ teaspoon salt**
> **8 (6-inch) corn tortillas**
> **1 tablespoon vegetable oil**
> **1 pound medium raw shrimp, peeled, deveined and chopped**
> **2 teaspoons chili powder**

1. Combine peach, onion, jalapeño, lime juice, parsley, garlic and salt in medium glass bowl. Set aside.

2. Preheat oven to 400°F. Cut out 24 rounds from tortillas using 2½-inch biscuit cutter or sharp knife. Drape tortilla rounds over handle of wooden spoon to make taco shells; secure with toothpicks. Bake 5 minutes; repeat with remaining tortilla rounds.

3. Heat oil in large nonstick skillet over medium-high heat. Add shrimp and chili powder; cook and stir 3 minutes or until shrimp are pink and opaque.

4. Place shrimp in taco shells; top with peach salsa.

Brie Bites

Spicy Polenta Cheese Bites

Makes 32 appetizers

   3 cups water
   1 cup corn grits or cornmeal
  ½ teaspoon salt
  ¼ teaspoon chili powder
   1 tablespoon butter
  ¼ cup minced onion or shallot
   1 tablespoon minced jalapeño pepper*
  ½ cup (2 ounces) shredded sharp Cheddar or fontina cheese

Jalapeño peppers can sting and irritate the skin, so wear rubber gloves when handling peppers and do not touch your eyes.

1. Grease 8-inch square baking pan. Bring water to a boil in large nonstick saucepan over high heat. Slowly add grits, stirring constantly. Reduce heat to low; cook and stir until grits are tender and water is absorbed. Stir in salt and chili powder. Remove from heat.

2. Melt butter in small saucepan over medium-high heat. Add onion and jalapeño; cook and stir 3 to 5 minutes or until tender. Stir into grits; mix well. Spread in prepared pan. Let stand 1 hour or until cool and firm.

3. Preheat broiler. Cut polenta into 16 squares. Arrange squares on nonstick baking sheet; sprinkle with cheese. Broil 4 inches from heat 5 minutes or until cheese is melted and slightly browned. Remove immediately. Cut squares in half. Serve warm or at room temperature.

For even spicier flavor, add ⅛ to ¼ teaspoon red pepper flakes to the onion-jalapeño mixture.

Spicy Polenta Cheese Bites

Ham & Cheese Quesadillas with Cherry Jam

Makes 4 servings

2 tablespoons vegetable oil
2 cups thinly sliced red onions
1 jalapeño pepper,* seeded and minced
2 cups pitted fresh sweet cherries
2 tablespoons packed brown sugar
2 teaspoons balsamic vinegar
½ teaspoon salt
4 (9-inch) flour tortillas
6 ounces ham, thinly sliced
4 ounces Havarti cheese, thinly sliced
2 teaspoons butter

Jalapeño peppers can sting and irritate the skin, so wear rubber gloves when handling peppers and do not touch your eyes.

1. Heat oil in large skillet over medium-high heat. Add onions and jalapeño; cook and stir 3 minutes or until onions are golden. Add cherries; cook and stir 1 minute. Stir in brown sugar, vinegar and salt. Cook over low heat 1 minute, stirring constantly. Remove from heat; cool slightly.

2. Arrange one fourth of ham slices and one fourth of cheese slices over one side of each tortilla. Top with 2 tablespoons cherry jam. Fold tortillas in half. Set aside remaining jam.

3. Melt 1 teaspoon butter in large skillet over medium heat. Add 2 quesadillas; press down firmly with spatula. Cook 3 to 4 minutes per side or until golden and cheese melts. Remove from skillet. Repeat with remaining quesadillas. Cut quesadillas in half. Serve with reserved cherry jam.

Ham & Cheese Quesadillas with Cherry Jam

Index

Measurements

1 teaspoon = ⅙ ounce

1½ teaspoons = ½ tablespoon = ¼ ounce

1 tablespoon = 3 teaspoons = ½ ounce

2 tablespoons = 6 teaspoons = 1 ounce

¼ cup = 4 tablespoons = 2 ounces

½ cup = 8 tablespoons = 4 ounces

¾ cup = 12 tablespoons = 6 ounces

1 cup = 16 tablespoons = ½ pint = 8 ounces

2 cups = 1 pint = 16 ounces

METRIC CONVERSION CHART

VOLUME MEASUREMENTS (dry)

$1/8$ teaspoon = 0.5 mL
$1/4$ teaspoon = 1 mL
$1/2$ teaspoon = 2 mL
$3/4$ teaspoon = 4 mL
1 teaspoon = 5 mL
1 tablespoon = 15 mL
2 tablespoons = 30 mL
$1/4$ cup = 60 mL
$1/3$ cup = 75 mL
$1/2$ cup = 125 mL
$2/3$ cup = 150 mL
$3/4$ cup = 175 mL
1 cup = 250 mL
2 cups = 1 pint = 500 mL
3 cups = 750 mL
4 cups = 1 quart = 1 L

VOLUME MEASUREMENTS (fluid)

1 fluid ounce (2 tablespoons) = 30 mL
4 fluid ounces ($1/2$ cup) = 125 mL
8 fluid ounces (1 cup) = 250 mL
12 fluid ounces ($1 1/2$ cups) = 375 mL
16 fluid ounces (2 cups) = 500 mL

WEIGHTS (mass)

$1/2$ ounce = 15 g
1 ounce = 30 g
3 ounces = 90 g
4 ounces = 120 g
8 ounces = 225 g
10 ounces = 285 g
12 ounces = 360 g
16 ounces = 1 pound = 450 g

DIMENSIONS

$1/16$ inch = 2 mm
$1/8$ inch = 3 mm
$1/4$ inch = 6 mm
$1/2$ inch = 1.5 cm
$3/4$ inch = 2 cm
1 inch = 2.5 cm

OVEN TEMPERATURES

250°F = 120°C
275°F = 140°C
300°F = 150°C
325°F = 160°C
350°F = 180°C
375°F = 190°C
400°F = 200°C
425°F = 220°C
450°F = 230°C

BAKING PAN SIZES

Utensil	Size in Inches/Quarts	Metric Volume	Size in Centimeters
Baking or	$8 \times 8 \times 2$	2 L	$20 \times 20 \times 5$
Cake Pan	$9 \times 9 \times 2$	2.5 L	$23 \times 23 \times 5$
(square or	$12 \times 8 \times 2$	3 L	$30 \times 20 \times 5$
rectangular)	$13 \times 9 \times 2$	3.5 L	$33 \times 23 \times 5$
Loaf Pan	$8 \times 4 \times 3$	1.5 L	$20 \times 10 \times 7$
	$9 \times 5 \times 3$	2 L	$23 \times 13 \times 7$
Round Layer	$8 \times 1 1/2$	1.2 L	20×4
Cake Pan	$9 \times 1 1/2$	1.5 L	23×4
Pie Plate	$8 \times 1 1/4$	750 mL	20×3
	$9 \times 1 1/4$	1 L	23×3
Baking Dish	1 quart	1 L	—
or Casserole	$1 1/2$ quart	1.5 L	—
	2 quart	2 L	—